MW01171264

Why B Flat When you can "C" Sharp
Copyright © 2021 Jonathan L. Brown

Prepared for Publication by Brown House Media

Cover Design ©2021 by Brown House Media

Library of Congress Control Information Available
Paperback ISBN 10: 1637908059
Paperback ISBN 13: 9781637908051

First Edition
Printed in the United States of America

Unless otherwise noted, scriptural references are taken from the King James Version of the Bible.

Table of Contents

Chapters:

Sight is the Enemy of Vision

You're too Big for a rear-view mirror

The Power of Keys

Don't believe what you can't see

There's nothing wrong with you

Wake up

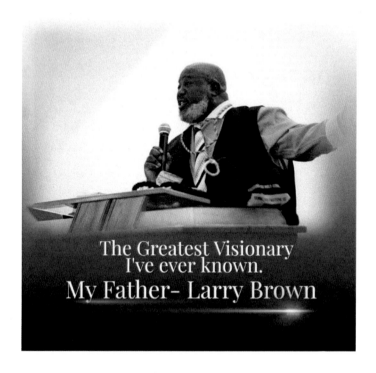

The Greatest Visionary
I've ever known.
My Father- Larry Brown

1956 - 2020

Chapter 1

Sight is the Enemy of Vision!

The ability to see is an attribute of our human nature that most individuals take for granted. Out of the five natural senses that we all possess including "taste, smell, touch, and hearing, the ability to see is probably the most powerful. Our eyes are the gateway by which we see the entire world. They are also the platform for us to build a unique perception of life. It does not matter what race you are nor your economic social status. Everybody has a different perception of life depending on how they view the world. It wasn't until I truly started to understand this process that I realized just because you can see doesn't mean you have vision!

A study of statistics from "The Global Burden of Vision Impairment Agency" stated that there are 7.3 billion people in the world. Out of those 7 billion people, 253 million people are visually impaired and 37 Million are blind! Even though that leaves over 6 billion people with the ability to see, what if I told you that many of them have no vision?

Sight is defined as:

The power or faculty of seeing; perception by the eyes; vision. 2. the act or an instance of seeing. 3. the range of vision: within sight of land. 4. range of mental vision; point of view; judgment: Something that is seen 5: the process, power, or function of seeing specifically: one of the five basic physical senses by which light stimuli received by the eye are interpreted by the brain and constructed into a representation of the position, shape, brightness, and usually color of objects in space.

I personally know hundreds of people that can see but have absolutely "POOR" vision! I know that seems like an oxymoron, but let's think about a few things for a second.

Have you ever asked yourself, what do people see when they look at you? To some individuals it may not matter, but remember perception is often based off what people initially see.

Take into consideration these visual facts:

- The brain can see images that last for just 13 milliseconds.
- Our eyes can register 36,000 visual messages per hour.
- We can get the sense of a visual scene in less than 1/10 of a second.
- 90% of information transmitted to the brain is visual.
- Visuals are processed 60,000 times faster in the brain than text.
- 40% of nerve fibers are linked to the eye retina.

Perception

That brings a whole different narrative to the phrase "What do you see?"

Before people ever hear you, they see you! When people are turned off by what they see, it automatically makes them prejudice to what they hear. - JBrowniePoint

Now I know you don't want to believe that, but let's be honest for a second. How many times have you seen a homeless person on the street? Probably more times than you can count right? And what were your initial thoughts when you saw them? Most of us would have to admit that we had a preconceived judgement of them simply based off what they looked like. We don't give them an opportunity to hold a conversation with us because subconsciously we're already turned off by what we see. Ironically, that's probably why most homeless people just simply hold up a sign for you to read because they already know you won't talk to them! And even by chance they do speak and ask, "Can you spare some change?", most of us would say no and keep going. Why do we do that? It's simple, your perception of what you see makes you prejudice to anything they could possibly say. Have you ever stopped to ask them their story? How did they end up homeless? What life skills or professional skills do they have? If you're like me, your answer is probably not. That all changed for me a few years ago. When my family lived in Orlando Florida my dad used to work at the men's homeless shelter.

Whenever I would go up to visit him at his job, I would see countless numbers of homeless men. They were a mix of all different ages and races. At first, like many people I didn't want to be around them. I thought they were dirty, smelt bad, and simply regarded them as less than me. After a while I began to feel sorry for them and wanted to know how they ended up like this. What happened to you? Where is your family? How did you end up here in life? To my surprise, I was absolutely shocked at some of their stories! Some of them were extremely educated with professional skillsets. One guy I met was a former accountant, and another was an attorney. I even met one guy that was a doctor! Can you believe that? This guy had a whole M.D. behind his name but was laying on a mat everyday in a homeless shelter. When I asked how they got to the place of being homeless their answers were heartbreaking. The lawyer said, "I lost my family in a car accident and gave up on life." The accountant said, "I started using drugs and lost my business." The most heartbreaking was the doctor who said, "My wife was murdered, and I simply fell into depression because I no longer cared about anything in life!"

Looking back on when I initially saw them, I didn't care what skills they had because I'd already formed a preconceived perception of them based off what I saw. This applies to many areas in life. Always remember this....

Your skills are not determined by your appearance, but your appearance can determine the opportunities given to your skills! - JBrowniePoint

This is the problem with sight vs the power of vision. The struggle with most individuals dealing with any issues begins with what they see. Often times what we see today reflects distorted vision. Everybody looks the same. Your identity is based on what you see around you and not what you see inside of you. This now becomes problematic for your future.

The Power of Vision

Up until now I've given you some practical principles to apply. Now, let us look at this from a Biblical point of view.

NIV Bible Mark 8:22-26

22 They came to Bethsaida, and some people brought a blind man and begged Jesus to touch him. 23 He took the blind man by the hand and led him outside the village. When he had spit on the man's eyes and put his hands on him, Jesus asked, "Do you see anything?" 24 He looked up and said, "I see people; they look like trees walking around." 25 Once more Jesus put his hands on the man's eyes. Then his eyes were opened, his sight was restored, and he saw everything clearly. 26 Jesus sent him home, saying, "Don't even go into[a] the village."

In this passage of scripture Jesus heals a man that was blind. Notice that the first thing Jesus did was lead him away from the village. This is controversial because everyone knows that its dangerous to take a blind person away from their place of familiarity. Even though they can't see, they become accustomed to their surroundings and familiarize themselves with a routine that provides safety. But before Jesus could change his vision, he had to first change his setting! People have difficulty changing because of what they constantly see around them in life. Unfortunately, sometimes the only way to change what you see is to change where you are! The scripture then says that Jesus spit on the man's eyes and put his hands on him. Jesus then asked what the man saw. The man replied by saying "I see men walking like trees." Although he could see, his vision was still distorted. Notice after the man said he saw men as trees that Jesus laid hands on him again. Biblically this is a very crucial point! What makes this crucial is because, this is the only time recorded in the Bible where Jesus had to touch somebody twice to heal them is when he's changing their vision!

Let me ask you a controversial question. Have you ever met a homosexual that was born blind? Really think about that for minute. Have you ever met a lesbian that was born blind? More than likely your answer will be no. Do you know why? It's hard to become something you can't see! If I can't see it, then it's hard for me to become it. Now I know that may be controversial for some of you, but that's the power of vision vs sight.

In the last verse of the scripture, after Jesus healed the man's vision, he told him do not go back to the village. Why would he say that? The answer is simple. Never go back to people that catered to your blindness when God has given you perfect vision?

As I said in the beginning of this chapter, there are millions of people that can see but that doesn't mean they have vision. One thing I've learned in life is knowing the difference between sight and vision is the key to your success. Sight is not vision and vision is not sight! Let me break it down.

Sight is an external view of your current position, resources, and situation. Vision is an internal promise that God gave you! - JBrowniePoint

Your sight is the enemy of your vision because many times what you see won't match up with what God promised you! You can't get distracted or discouraged by what you see. If God gave you a vision, it doesn't matter what obstacles you face in life. Trust your vision and ignore your sight.

Write the Vision.

Whenever you start talking about anything dealing with vision to spiritual people, they almost immediately always reference Habakkuk 2:2 in the Bible. Basically, it says "Write the vision and make it plain." Being that I'm a "PK" (Preacher's Kid), I grew up hearing this a thousand times in church. It wasn't until I got older and started studying the power of vision that I found out there's much more to that scripture. We always start at verse 2, but the true power of vision is found in verse 1. Here is what is says.

Habakkuk 2:1 King James Version (KJV) I will stand upon my watch, and set me upon the tower, and will watch to see what he will say unto me, and what I shall answer when I am reproved.

That one verse changed my whole perspective on vision. It starts off by saying "I will stand upon my watch." Well, this deals with duty, time, and authority. If you know anything about military protocol, to stand on your watch means to stand in a position and guard. It also means to watch someone or something to look for possible danger and threats. In order to fully understand the power of vison in this verse, you need to first ask yourself who was Habakkuk?

Habakkuk was a prophet whose oracles and prayer are recorded in the Book of Habakkuk. He was the eighth of the collected twelve minor prophets in the Hebrew Bible. He identified himself as "Habakkuk the prophet" (Habakkuk 1:1; 3:1), a term that indicates Habakkuk was a professional prophet. This meant that Habakkuk was trained in the Law of Moses in a prophetic school, an institution for educating prophets that came after the days of Samuel (1 Samuel 19:20; 2 Kings 4:38).

Now that we know Habakkuk was a prophet, this gives more power to his ability to see when he said, "I will stand upon my watch." Prophets in the Bible were always represented as watchmen, watching constantly for the comfort, safety, and welfare of the people. They were also watching to receive information from the Lord. Like many prophets today, the prophetic influence was not always with them, but was granted only at particular times, according to the will of God. When Habakkuk said I will stand upon my watch, that meant he had authority as a prophet to use his vision to safeguard against the enemy. The next line in that scripture said, "and set me upon the tower." This meant that he was in an elevated position to have the advantage of a further range of vision. If your vision doesn't surpass your sight, then you haven't looked hard enough! Your vision should always have a further range than your natural ability to see. The question now becomes what do you see?

The most pivotal line in that first verse of scripture says, "and will watch to see what he will say unto me." This seems ridiculous because nobody ever watches to see what you're saying. They listen to what you're saying! If someone is talking to you, you can't see their words, you can only hear their words! But in this verse Habakkuk said, "I will watch to see what he will say unto me." Shouldn't he have said I will listen to hear what he will say unto me? That would certainly seem more rational to me, but that's not what he said. He said I will watch to see what he will say unto me. This now means that words have the power to speak life to vision. Have you ever heard the phrase "You have to see it before you see it, or you never will see it." That means the manifestation of what you will ultimately see in the natural begins with what you speak in your vision.

Now you're ready for verse 2 that says:

And the LORD answered me, and said, Write the vision, and make it plain upon tables, that he may run that readeth it.

Remember that your vison is based on your words and not what you see. You have to write it down. You may be saying well what do I write? It's simple, you write words! It's not rocket science! You can't go by what you see naturally because your sight is the enemy of your vision. Write down what's in your heart. What did God promise you? If God spoke something to you then that means He used words. When you write words down it gives life to your vision. The last part of that scripture says:

For the vision is yet for an appointed time, but at the end it shall speak, and not lie: though it tarry, wait for it; because it will surely come, it will not tarry.

This means that although you may not see it now, that doesn't mean it's not going to happen. Your vision will happen at the appointed time. Here's something you should remember. Whenever God gives you a vision, He always shows you the end result. He never shows you the beginning. For example, if God gives you a vision for a successful hair salon with 20 employees in a downtown prime location with celebrity clients… That's the end result. Trust me, you're not going to start off like that. You have to go through the process. That process may begin with you starting out doing people's hair from your kitchen at first. That's why it's so important that you write it down. Because during the time of your process you can't afford to forget the vision! Even if you get discouraged during the process and feel like giving up, go back and read your vision. Don't let what you see during your process forfeit what He promised you in your vision. This is where most people end up developing what I call "POOR" vision.

Passing
Over
Opportunities
Repeatedly

Sometimes because what you see doesn't match your vision, you end up passing over opportunities that are available to actually help you with your vision. For example, earlier I used a successful hair salon as a point of reference for someone that has a vision. If you're starting out doing hair from your kitchen, but an established hair salon offers you a job in their salon washing hair, that's not an opportunity you need to pass up. The reason is simple. That's an opportunity for you to learn everything you need to know from an established salon on how to run your own! It doesn't matter if you're a great stylist. If all they want you to do is wash hair then wash hair. But make sure while you're washing hair that you're also learning how they do business, what attracts their clients, what products do they use, and everything else that makes them successful.

The success of your vision is predicated on what you learn during your process. – JBbrowniePoint

During your process don't develop "POOR" vision by passing over opportunities repeatedly that could form a foundation for the success of your vision.

The Black Widow Spider

I'm the type of person that loves nature. I'm always watching Discovery Channel and intrigued by things that happen in the animal kingdom. One day I was sitting at home watching a documentary on spiders. On this particular day the show featured the Black Widow Spider. I was absolutely blown away by what I learned about spiders and their vision. Contrary to what we've seen in movies, spider vision isn't a superhero trait. Ironically, most spiders have very poor eyesight despite having 8 eyes (some have more than eight, some less than six) especially those that wait for their prey in fixed locations. Other than detecting swift motion, their spider vision can do nothing more than spotting changes in the environmental light intensity. This function exists so that they can know when it's time to do their nocturnal activities such as hunting, weaving their web or shift location. Black widow spiders are arachnids that are known for the female's unique appearance and tendency to eat their mates. That's right, I said eat their mates! They're considered the most venomous spiders in North America. Even more amazing is that for the most part, the female Black Widow spider is basically blind. Male and female black widows look different. In all cases, "the females are the most distinctive, with shiny black bodies and a red hourglass-shaped marking on the underside of their round abdomen. The female is twice the size of the male. Like many spiders, the black widow spider eats other spiders and insects that get caught in their webs. The female spider hangs upside down from her web motionless as she waits for her prey. Because she can't see, she has to wait until she feels movement in the web to attack her prey. Here's where things get crazy.

During mating season, the male widow spider will capture a live insect and bring it to the female's web. She's twice his size and because she can't see, he brings a live moving insect to distract her while feeding so he can mate with her. What happens next blew my mind. After mating with the female, the male lays in the web to rest. By this time the female has finished eating her prey that the male brought her. She can't see so she doesn't know the male is still laying motionless in her web. When the male finally decides to leave, the female senses movement in her web. Because she can't see, she responds to any movement as prey that's been caught in her web. She kills her mate and in doing so ends up killing the very thing that's there to secure her future all because she has no vision! Ultimately, she ends up giving birth to another generation of visionless babies.

Visionless people will always threaten the security of their future by always responding to every little thing they feel. – JBrowniePoint

Chapter 2

You're too Big for a rear-view mirror.

Being a parent can be one of the most amazing experiences anyone could have. But like anything else, parenting has its challenges too. The funny thing is, when you're growing up you don't realize some of the stress you put your parents through. I remember when I became a teenager the first thing I wanted to do was get my driver's license. I mean I couldn't wait! It was all I cared about. I didn't own a car or a scooter, but none of that mattered. Like most kids, I just wanted a license so I could brag to all my friends about being able to drive. Not to mention, it also helped boost your chances with the ladies if you were actually able to drive on a date.

I remember my dad taking me into an empty parking lot to teach me how to drive. Boy was I excited! Back then my dad had a brand-new Cadillac Fleetwood Brougham. It was black with a smooth rag top and chrome panels. That thing was as big as a boat, but I didn't care. I was ready to drive off like the pros. Even though the parking lot was empty, my dad made me act like it was packed full of cars. He even put a few cones out to represent cars at certain times.

One of the first things he did was teach me how to park. He would say things like, "Don't turn too wide", and "Make sure you don't swipe the side of the other car!" I thought this was all crazy because remember, there was nobody else in the parking lot. It was just us. But yet and still, he was shouting out, "Hey watch it! Don't hit that car!"

After a while, I got pretty good at pulling in and parking. Once my dad saw that I knew how to pull in and park, he started teaching me how to back in and parallel park. This is when I first learned the power of mirrors.

Set up to look back

As the years went by, I grew into adulthood and became a fairly good driver. I've mastered all the initial training my father taught me and even learned a few tricks of my own. I've been all over the country and driven on countless roads in many states. I think I'm pretty good if you ask me.

On an average, I usually travel on a weekly basis for work. The cities may vary, but the job is still the same. It doesn't matter if I'm teaching a Masterclass, speaking at a conference, or performing; I can pretty much guarantee that I'll have to travel to do it. One night while I was driving home on the interstate, there was a guy driving a car behind me that ran up on me and turned on his high beam lights. If you're like me, I can't stand when drivers do that! I was already doing 75mph and here comes this crazy guy doing 85mph that wants me to move over. All I could see in my rear-view mirror was his high beams which were blinding me!

It didn't matter how much I tried to focus on the road ahead of me, all I could see was this guy's high beams blasting my eyes from the rear-view mirror. Eventually I just moved over and let him pass me. I continued my drive home, but I kept thinking about how that guy irritated me with his high beams. I was so frustrated that I said to myself, I wish I could take this rear-view mirror off! It was during that very moment that a thought came to mind. Why do we even have rear-view mirrors? Did you know that the average size dimensions for a car windshield are 59 inches by 31.5 inches? That's literally 5 feet wide and almost 3 feet high. But the average standard sizes for a car rear-view mirror are 8-inch, 10-inch, and 12-inch.

When you actually sit and think about it, that's crazy! Why would you take a small view of what's behind me and place it right in the middle of a larger view of what's in front of me? Think about that for a second. You have a large clear view of the road ahead of you, but yet right in the middle of that is a small reflection of what you've already passed behind you!

It's dangerous to keep looking at the small things you've already passed when there's a bigger view of what's coming ahead of you! – JBbrowniePoint

This is one of the biggest setbacks to anyone's vision when trying to achieve purpose. Don't keep looking back at what you've already passed. If you've already passed it, why keep reflecting on it? It took me a long time to figure this out. Just like many individuals, I've made more mistakes than I can count. When I first started doing motivational speaking and music Masterclasses, I was my own biggest hinderance. I kept thinking about all the mistakes I made in life and the repeated failures I experienced. I mean who would really want to listen to me talk? I've been a failure more than I've been a success. My mind wasn't focused on the bigger picture because I always had past reflections. Everybody has a rear-view mirror in their life. You can't afford to keep putting a past image in the middle of your forward vision! Contrary to what we've been taught, there's something I learned.

Failure is not the opposite of success, it's a part of success. – JBrowniePoint

Just like the guy that drove up behind me and turned on his high beams, you have to be careful of people that are an opportunist. It doesn't matter to them that you're on the same road heading in the same direction. They just want to force you out of their way so they can pass you. You're both heading in the same direction, but that doesn't matter. An opportunist will use any advantage to pass you just to say they got there before you.

It's funny how life plays out sometimes. A little while later I ended up passing that same guy that had his high beams on. He was pulled over on the side of the road with a flat tire! As I got closer to him, I slowed down just enough for him to see me. The look on his face was priceless! I know that sounds petty of me, but isn't it funny how people react when they don't see you in the last place they left you!

U-Haul Trucks

Despite everything I've tried to convey in this chapter concerning rear-view mirrors and the correlation of forward vision, every car has one. I guess in reality the automobile manufacturers wouldn't put them in there if you didn't need them, right? I used to think the same thing until one day I had to move. When I first got married, me and my wife were living in a one-bedroom apartment. It wasn't very big in there and if you know anything about women, she had way more stuff than me! My wife had so many clothes I couldn't believe it. Before marrying me, my wife lived in a much larger 3-bedroom apartment. She ended up downsizing and putting the majority of her things in storage two years before we got married. After we got settled, we decided to get a bigger place. Of course, she was extremely happy because that meant she could finally get her things out of storage. On the day we were set to move, I went to rent a truck from U-Haul. We had a lot of things to move so I got a 26-foot truck. When I got in the truck and got ready to leave, I noticed something very strange. There was no rear-view mirror! I thought to myself, maybe it fell down or was broken. I got out of the truck and started to go inside to tell the manager, but as I was walking back to the office, I noticed none of the trucks had rearview mirrors. This was puzzling to me.

Why hadn't I ever noticed this before? Were all U-Haul trucks like this? Eventually, I got back in the truck and drove off. As I was driving, I couldn't shake the weird feeling of not having a rear-view mirror to look at. I was so used to having one in my car that it just felt strange. After a while, I looked around and noticed something. It really wouldn't matter if I had one anyway because there was nothing to see behind me! There was no window behind me and even if there was, the trailer of the truck was so big that it blocked my view of anything I could possibly see. I continued home and finished moving our things. As time went on, I started to think. How many other trucks don't have rear-view mirrors? Was it just U-Haul?

During my research I started studying 18-wheeler trucks. As you know, they're the biggest thing on the road. The tractor itself usually has 10 wheels and is around 20-25 feet long. When it's connected to a trailer it becomes a tractor-trailer combination vehicle with 18 wheels. The trailer is about 53 feet long. That's pretty big! Despite their size, I found out that no 18-wheeler truck has rear-view mirrors. What? Are you serious? This was crazy to me. How come it's mandatory for me to have one in my little car but they don't need one in their huge truck? With estimates of 2,752,043 tractor-trailers on the road out of a total of 268 million licensed drivers, the odds point to tractor-trailers as some of the most dangerous vehicles on the road.

According to the **Federal Motor Carrier Safety Administration**, in the year 2018... 4,761 people were killed in crashes involving large trucks, of which 3,289 involved tractor-trailers or combination trucks. That means 69% of accidents resulting in fatalities involved tractor-trailers. This furthermore made me ask the question, why don't they have rear-view mirrors? It was in my studying of accident reports that I found the answer.

Big Loads Require Sharp Vision

Did you know that the weight of your average motor vehicle is about 2.5 tons, while a tractor trailer can weigh 40 tons? It takes much longer to stop a tractor-trailer than a motor vehicle. For example, if a vehicle and a tractor-trailer are both driving at 40 mph and start braking at the same moment, the tractor-trailer will travel 45 feet further before coming to a complete stop. While a passenger car needs about 306 feet to stop after braking, a tractor-trailer needs 525 feet. That's about the length of 1.5 football fields. Speed is also an important factor when applying the brakes. The faster a vehicle is traveling, the longer it takes to stop. Because of the size and weight of a big truck, the odds of a fatality in a truck accident are more dangerously common. Big trucks don't need a rearview mirror because what they're carrying is too big to look back.

Always focus your vision on what's ahead of you and remember the weight you carry behind you.
– JBrowniePoint

What you're carrying is bigger than the average load. This is key for every leader to understand. Your vision must be fixed on the road ahead without the reflection of what's behind you. The moment you get distracted could be fatal for everyone around you. I know others may seem like they're moving ahead faster in life, but that's because they're smaller too. Your dreams, passions, and desires are bigger, so you can't afford to go as fast. Sometimes the people around you don't have the capacity to carry the same weight as you. Because they're smaller, it's easier for them to move in and out of situations that you can't because of the size of what you're carrying. You're simply too big to be that reckless. Sure, small cars are much faster, but big trucks can go further. The average gas tank size for cars is 12 gallons. Larger cars hold up to 16 gallons, and the smallest tanks can hold around 9 gallons. An 18-wheeler truck uses diesel. The tanks can hold anywhere from 60 gallons to 200 gallons each. Most trucks have a tank on each side so if they're 200-gallon tanks, the 18-wheeler can carry 400 gallons of fuel when full. Smaller cars are designed to go a short distance at quick speed while big trucks are designed to go a long distance at a steady speed.

Just because they're faster than you doesn't mean they have the capacity to keep up with you! – JBrowniePoint

The proof of your success is always measured by your longevity. You can't get distracted by people that get to certain points in life quicker than you. Remember, because of your size, you're designed to go a further distance which means it's going to take longer to get there. The road to success is filled with adversity. How much adversity you experience depends on which vehicle you decide to take. If you want to have something quick that probably won't last as long because you keep reflecting on what's behind you instead of the road in front of you, take the car. But if you know that what you're carrying inside of you is much bigger and you truly have the capacity to go much further in life, take the 18- wheeler. Always keep your vision focused on the road ahead. No matter how many individuals around you are looking at past reflections while driving on the road to success, remember you're simply too big for a rear-view mirror!

Chapter 3

The Power of Keys

Music has always been a part of my life. I was born into a family of singers and musicians. My father was a skilled saxophonist, and my mother was a great singer. My grandparents were singers and nearly all my cousins are musicians. Music is just in our blood. I first started playing piano at the age of seven. I wasn't very good, but the pressure was already on me to exceed everybody's musical expectations. Remember, everyone in my family was a skilled musician. Some of them weren't simply good, they were amazing! This made things challenging for me because the bar of excellence they set often seemed too hard for me to reach. In the late 80's, my father started pastoring a small church in Algood Tennessee. It was during this time that I really took an interest in music.

I can remember many days sitting up listening to songs on the radio and trying figure out how to play them. Even though my father was a saxophonist, he also knew how to play a little bit of piano. He tried to teach me what he could from time to time, but it just wasn't enough. That all changed after one embarrassing Sunday morning at church.

I remember one Sunday my father got up to sing an old hymn. As he began to sing the second stanza of the hymn, he motioned for me to modulate the song to another key. I was fine with the first key that he was singing in because I was fluent in that key. But I couldn't modulate when he asked me to take it up because I couldn't play in the next key. My father stopped in the middle of the song and said in the microphone, "What's wrong, you can't play in that key?" I was so embarrassed! How could he do this to me on a Sunday morning in the middle of service in front of a church full of people? As my father stood there in the pulpit waiting for my response, I had to shamefully say, "No, I can't play in that key."

My father then turned and said to the audience, "My son can't play in that key so we're going to sing the song in a key he can play in." I was so embarrassed that I could've crawled under a rock. My father then told the congregation, "We're going to sing this same song next Sunday and modulate it twelve times. And because Jon is going home with me, I'm going to make sure he learns how to play this song in every key this week!" If that seems harsh for a father to treat his son like that in front of people, remember my whole family was musicians, and they had a high standard set for me. My father understood the value of mastering your craft. As I came home from school that Monday afternoon, my father was waiting for me downstairs in our house.

"Do you know why I did that to you yesterday at church?" with tears in my eyes I looked at him and said, "No." He then said to me, "I don't ever want you to miss an opportunity because you're unprepared for the moment."

It's better to be prepared and not have an opportunity than to have an opportunity and not be prepared!
— JBrowniePoint

He made me practice every day until I could play that song in every key. This became my normal routine. Go to school, come home, and do my homework. Then right after my homework, I had to practice the piano. When school let out for the summer, my dad decided to do something that I didn't expect. He sent me to stay the entire summer with my cousin Joe in Knoxville. Joe was one of the best musicians in our family. My dad's instructions were simple. I wasn't allowed to go swimming, play at the parks, play video games, or anything else that most kids looked forward to doing during the summer break. He sent me to stay with my cousin Joe during the summer for training. That's right, training! Every summer my dad would send me off to stay with one of my relatives who were skilled in music to train me. The objective was for me to come home 3 times better than I left. It was during these summer training sessions that I first learned the power of keys.

There are two ways you can define a key. It all depends on the type of key and the purpose it is designed for.

One definition of a key is:

A small piece of shaped metal with incisions cut to fit the wards of a particular lock, which is inserted into a lock and turned to open or close it. A small, shaped metal implement for operating a switch in the form of a lock, especially one operating the ignition of a motor vehicle. A lever depressed by the finger in playing an instrument such as the organ, piano, flute, or concertina: a group of notes based on a particular note and comprising a scale, regarded as forming the tonal basis of a piece or passage of music.

Basically, this means that keys have two distinct functions…to sound and to unlock.

In music, keys are the foundation by which everything is created. It doesn't matter what instrument you play, in order for you to create a sound there must be keys. In our normal daily functions, we use keys to lock and unlock doors. But what if I told you that your life is filled with different keys waiting to be used to open unimaginable doors?

A key in your life is just like a noun. It can be a person, place, or thing! This is crucial to identifying valuable assets that come in your life in the form of a key. For instance, sometimes a person can be the vital key needed to open a huge door in your life. On the other hand, when it comes to business sometimes location is the key to your success. No matter what your vision is, you must identify the keys around you to maximize your potential.

House vs Key

As a young child growing up in my parents' house, I never really understood the concept of rules and responsibilities. It wasn't until later in my teenage years that my father decided to test me in responsibility. He did this by simply giving me a key to the house. At the time, I had absolutely no idea of the value that came along with having a key to my father's house nor the responsibility. I was just simply glad to have my own key. Finally, I didn't have to wait for somebody to come home to let me in. I had my own key! I could simply come and go as I pleased. But I would soon find out the true measure of responsibility that came along with that key and the value that it held. I remember one day hanging out with a group of my friends. It was just like any other day. We were laughing, having fun and just simply enjoying the day. But later that evening, as I began to head home, I realized I didn't have my key. Where did I put it? What happened to it? And most of all, what was I going to tell my father? I already knew this was going to be a problem because it took him so long to give me a key in the first place. The closer I got to the house, the more I began to think about what I was going to say to Daddy. But then I thought, well, maybe it won't be that bad. After all, it's just a key. Maybe he'll give me another one. Just as I began walking in the yard to the house, my dad pulled up in the driveway. My father worked late evenings, but on this particular day he came home early. I tried to throw him off by striking up a conversation. Hey there, what are you doing home early? How was your day? You need help getting anything out of the car? He looked at me with this confused look on his face like he knew something was up. He said "No, I'm OK, but go in the house and bring me my tool bag." I said, huh? He said, "Go in the house and bring me my tool bag out of the room." I stood there almost frozen in a daze. He said, "what's wrong with you?" I said I don't have my key.

He said, "what do you mean? You don't have your key? What happened to it?" I looked at him and said I think I lost it. He shook his head in disappointment and said, I just gave you that key. After that he told me to get in the car. As he was driving, I noticed that we pulled up at the Home Depot store. When we got inside, he took me over to the key station. Now as a kid, I'd been in Home Depot before with my father, but I never noticed the key station. He took out his keys and told the man standing behind the counter that he wanted to make a new key. The man took my father's house key and put it into the machine and made a new copy. When we got to the checkout counter, the lady swiped the price of the new key and said that'll be $3. My father paid for the key and we walked back to the car. When we got back to the house, he put the car on park and handed me the new key. But before I got out of the car, he turned and said something very important to me. He said, "don't lose this key. You are responsible for what this key gives you access to."

It wasn't until later in life that I figured out the true measure of what he was saying in that statement. You see, I watched him pay $3 for that key. So, in my eyes, there wasn't much value to it. I mean, it was just the key. A small little $3 key. If I lost it again, I could simply replace it with little to no cost. What was the big deal? It was just a key. It wasn't until I became an adult and purchased my own home that I realized the true value of a key is not in its price. The real value of any key is in what it gives you access to. You see it takes a $3 key to give you access to $1,000,000 house. The price of the key is meaningless, but the value of what it gives you access to is priceless.

Even though keys are small, the size of opportunities they give you access to is enormous!

Small hinges always swing Big Doors! – JBbrowniePoint

When it comes to business, one of the things that many successful individuals always teach is to create a vision board. Vision boards are usually filled with opportunities and life goals that people want to accomplish. Everybody's vision board is different. Goals are easy to identify in life because they are usually preceded by a door of opportunity. The problem is most people can't identify the small hinges that are key to swinging open those big doors. When it comes to vision, it's much easier for people to see something big in the distance rather than pay attention to something small up close. Understanding this concept is key to your success in life. God will always disguise a big opportunity in a small moment. We often pray for God to bless us with a big Oak tree blessing. And God often responds by giving us an acorn. You say, Lord, that's not what I asked for. I want the big Oak tree. And God responds by saying, I gave you an acorn. You see, within the acorn is the Oak tree. All you have to do is plant it and give it time to grow. Time is a major key to success that many individuals try to skip over. Whenever God gives you a vision, it's never the beginning. It's always the end picture that he shows you. It's up to you to identify the keys along the way to get you to the end result of what he showed you. For instance, if God showed you a vision of you owning a large construction company, then you probably need to start buying tools and learning how to build something. Why would you expect God to give you an enormous blessing and you haven't identified the necessary keys along the way to maintain that blessing? It just doesn't make sense.

Remember the power of any key is not in its size, but what it gives you access to. Identifying the right keys are crucial to your success in life. It doesn't matter how big the door is for any house, building, or dream that you may have. If you don't have the right key to open it, then you'll never gain access.

Chapter 4

Don't Believe what you can't see!

Growing up as a kid, I would always hear people say, "Don't believe everything you see!" I guess it was their way of teaching us not to be fooled by everything we saw. Some would even say things like, everything that glitter ain't gold. I understand the concept, but later I found out that is not necessarily true. As a matter of fact, I discovered later that it shouldn't be don't believe everything you see, but rather don't believe what you can't see. This is extremely hard for children to understand when it comes to being afraid of the dark. We've all been terrified of the dark at some point as kids. The fear comes their lack of vision. But contrary to what you think, children really aren't afraid of the dark because they can see that. What they're afraid of is what they can't see in the darkness! When it comes to vision, the feeling of thinking that there's something there that you can't see can be terrifying for anybody.

In dealing with your vision, your eyes often have an interesting way of playing tricks on you. Studies have shown that over 4 billion people wear glasses in the world. That's interesting being that the total world population is only 8 billion people. That means that over half of the people in the world have problems with their vision.

It's hard to be a great visionary and be short sighted at the same time. There are two types of people that have difficulty with vision. We typically label them in one of two classes. **Nearsighted** or **farsighted**. Understanding the range of your vision is equal to the potential of your success.
A *nearsighted* person sees close range objects clearly, while objects in the distance are blurred.

A *farsighted* person sees objects in the far distance clearly, while objects that are close are blurred.

These two impairments to your vision become crucial to the potential of your success in life. If you're a visionary that's nearsighted, then you focus on short term objectives and goals. The problem is you lack the ability to see long range. This is the main problem with overnight success stories. You're only focused on what you're able to see close range and never prepare for the change of what's coming in the future. A prime example of this are individuals that win the lottery. Most people are so engulfed with the hope of winning that they never stop to really plan. I mean think about that for a second. If you won $1,000,000 today, what would you do with it for the next 10 years? You can't expect someone who's never had any money to know what to properly do with money once they get it.

Domino and the Truck

Growing up as a kid, I always had a love for animals and nature. Oftentimes we would find street dogs in the neighborhood and bring them home to call them our own pets. My little sister was afraid of dogs at first, but eventually she began to love them. One day my father decided to buy us a real puppy of our own. He was a black and white border collie. We named him Domino because of the black and white spot patches in his fur. As a puppy, we kept him in the house, but as time went on, my mother made us put him outside. We had a pretty big backyard with plenty of space for him to run. The yard was fenced in, so we never had to worry about Domino running out in the street. Whenever me and my sister would go in the backyard to play kickball, Domino was extremely good at catching the ball. The way he would anticipate the ball going from one way to another was amazing to me. What I didn't realize is that Domino was a border collie. Border collies are classified as a working and herding type of dog breed. It was simply in his nature to chase things.

One day I let Domino out of the backyard. This particular day I decided that I wanted to play with Domino in the front yard so all my friends could see. He was a beautiful dog with black and white fur, and I wanted to show him off to everybody. While playing with him in the front yard, a big truck drove right by the house. Suddenly, out of nowhere, Domino took off running after the truck! I didn't know what to do. I was screaming Domino! Domino! Domino! It was too late. Domino had run halfway down the block chasing after that truck. When I finally caught up to Domino, I remember yelling at him saying what were you thinking? Why did you run after that truck? Get back over here! I couldn't believe he just took off running after the truck like that.

He had never done anything like this before. Even though I was upset, I was also scared because he could have gotten ran over. None of this mattered to Domino because all his vision was focused on was seeing the truck. That's the problem with nearsighted vision, you only focus on what you see close in front of you, not realizing what's in the distance. Even if Domino caught up with the truck, what could he do with it? Dogs can't drive! So, he was literally chasing something he couldn't handle if he got it.

Being farsighted is even worse because you have vision for the distance but can't see the steps in front of you in order to get there.

Sun...Moon... and Stars

I have a baby sister that's 3 years younger than me. As children, whenever we would play, my sister would sometimes run into the wall or sometimes doors while chasing me. Like any big brother, I would immediately stop running and ask her was she okay. She would say yes, and we'd continue playing. After a while my parents noticed that my sister started running into things more frequently. They took her to the doctor and sure enough, the doctor said, "she needs glasses." Upon testing my sister, they discovered that she was farsighted. I remember thinking to myself, how can she have the ability to see me across the room, but not see the table in front of her without tripping over it. When it comes to vision, being farsighted is really more of an illusion to your mind than a reality to your ability. Think about this for a moment. Everyday you wake up you can see the Sun in the sky. And every night you can see the Moon and Stars shining. But have you ever stopped to consider how far they are from you?

According to NASA, the Moon is an average of 238,855 miles away from Earth. The Sun is even further at an amazing 93 million miles away from Earth. It would literally take an airliner more than 20 years to fly that distance one way and that's traveling at 400 mph. If you think that's crazy check out the Stars!

The closest Star to our own is called "Proxima Centauri." Its 4.24 light-years away from Earth. In Deep Space it would take you 81,000 years to get there. To put that time scale into perspective, that would be over 2,700 human generations! This now makes it extremely difficult to believe someone's vision ability when you label them as farsighted. Here's the reason why. My sister had trouble seeing the table in front of her, but she could see the moon 238,855 miles away every night. How is it that the same eyes that can see the Sun 93 million miles away can't see the words in a book 12 inches in front of your face? It's the power of vision. That's why I titled this chapter "Don't believe what you can't see!" Because the reality is you have the ability within your vision to see much further than what they said you can't see. If you have the vision to see a Star over 2,700 generations away, then you certainly have more than enough ability to see the steps in front of you to get there.

Distorted Vision

As I mentioned in the first chapter, one of my favorite scriptures in the Bible is when Jesus healed the blind man who saw men as trees. Before Jesus could change his vision, he had to first change his setting. Sometimes people have a difficulty changing because of what they constantly see around them. Unfortunately, sometimes the only way to change what you see is to change where you are. The scripture says that Jesus spit on the man's eyes and put his hands on him. Jesus then asked the man, what do you see? Although he can see, his vision was still distorted. He saw men walking as trees. That's the challenge with distorted vision. Sometimes it's not what you see, but how you see. It's not just about seeing things, but also the perception of what it is that you're viewing. Take for instance sugar and salt. Side by side they look exactly the same in a bowl. The only thing that lets you know the difference is the package or container that it's placed in. How can you make effective decisions with distorted vision? Your judgment will always be negatively affected when your vision is distorted. Sometimes, in order for you to change your perception, you have to first ask the question, what distorted your vision? Even more importantly, who distorted your vision?

KJV Habakkuk 2:2 says:

² And the LORD answered me, and said, Write the vision, and make it plain upon tables, that he may run that readeth it.

You can't run with a vision that you can't see. So, the question is who distorted your vision? You may ask yourself; how do you know it's a person?
Have you read Galatians chapter 5 verse 7?

KJV Galatians 5:7 says:

⁷ Ye did run well; who did hinder you that ye should not obey the truth?

Sometimes the key to correcting your vision is to figure out who distorted it in the first place. Something happened in your life that changed the way you look at things. A bad relationship in your past can distort the way you view trust in the future. A broken heart caused by rejection can cause you to view someone's act of kindness as manipulation. No matter what happened or who happened to you in life, the road to purpose is always much clearer when you adjust your vision.

Chapter 5

There's Nothing Wrong with You!

Have you ever seen a possum play dead? For many people living in the city, this may be strange. But we grew up in the country. At night we would see all kinds of animals. Most of the time we would see deer and every once in a while, we'd see a skunk or fox. But the most interesting animal to see at night was a possum. Most people who see a possum are afraid. We would always try to scare the possum to watch it play dead. Whenever a possum plays dead, they lie on the ground motionless and seem to have no life. This defense mechanism is intended to confuse its attacker and allow the possum to escape. Many people believe it's a good act, but according to scientists the possum is actually in tonic immobility or thanatosis, and its body enters a catatonic state in response to fear. "Playing possum" isn't an act; it's an involuntary reaction to a threat.

Personally, I've used this particular act of playing possum on my sister many times. Whenever I didn't want to be bothered, I would just lay there and pretend like I was sleep. She knew I was faking, but it was my way of playing possum. Out of her frustration, she would often times shake me and say, "get up Jon ain't nothing wrong with you." I would still lay there like I was either dead or sleep. This was a fun game to play as kids, but as we got older, I realized there's still plenty of people playing possum in life.

You don't belong here.

One of the other stories I find interesting in the Bible is found in John Chapter 5. Most people who read it think it's about a man being healed. I personally think it's about a man who's become comfortable in a place he doesn't belong.

NIV John Chapter 5 verses 2-9

² Now there is in Jerusalem near the Sheep Gate a pool, which in Aramaic is called Bethesda and which is surrounded by five covered colonnades.

³ Here a great number of disabled people used to lie—the blind, the lame, the paralyzed. [4] [b] ⁵ One who was there had been an invalid for thirty-eight years.

⁶ When Jesus saw him lying there and learned that he had been in this condition for a long time, he asked him, "Do you want to get well?"

⁷ "Sir," the invalid replied, "I have no one to help me into the pool when the water is stirred. While I am trying to get in, someone else goes down ahead of me."

⁸ Then Jesus said to him, "Get up! Pick up your mat and walk." ⁹ At once the man was cured; he picked up his mat and walked.

The day on which this took place was a Sabbath, ¹⁰ and so the Jewish leaders said to the man who had been healed, "It is the Sabbath; the law forbids you to carry your mat."

¹¹ But he replied, "The man who made me well said to me, 'Pick up your mat and walk."

Whenever I would read this story in the Bible, I would always ask myself, why did Jesus pass everyone else just to speak to this one man? There were five porches filled with people who obviously needed a miracle. But yet, he passed all of them to speak to one man. Maybe he spoke to the man because he realized he was the only one who didn't belong there. Let's take a look at the people who the Bible said were in those five porches. It first starts off with the blind. This means they had no vision to even see the opportunity for a miracle. The second group of people the Bible mentions is the Lame. This group of people were physically crippled by injury and would take too long to reach a miracle. And the last group of people the Bible mentions is the paralyzed. These individuals have absolutely no hope of a miracle because they can't even move. It's interesting that out of all of the physical characteristics and inabilities of the people surrounding the 5 porches, this particular man has none of them. When Jesus saw him lying there, in a state of comfortability, He asked him a question. Do you want to get well? Amazingly, the man never even answered the question.

He just started giving excuses. But within his excuses, we find his truth. The man is not blind because he obviously can see Jesus talking to him. He's also not paralyzed because he responds with an excuse and says, "while I'm coming, somebody else steps down before me." This means that he can move. Otherwise, there would be no need to say someone steps down before me. Meaning I was on my way first, but they beat me to it. After reading this story over and over, I'm convinced that Jesus passed everyone else to speak to this man because he was the only one that didn't belong there. Out of everyone else that has a real problem, you're the only one out here that ain't nothing physically wrong with.

Many times, people have the ability to do better in life, but they've become comfortable with the handicaps of the people surrounding them. It's a dangerous thing to find comfort in someone else's discomfort. It all comes down to your perception and how you view life. Notice Jesus never healed the man in this particular story. He just simply asked him do you want to get better? The man never even answered the question. So, Jesus says, get up, take up your mat and walk. This may seem harsh, but it's actually a point of motivation. The mat is a source of comfortability that the man was lying on. So, when Jesus tells the man to pick up his mat and walk, what he's actually saying is, I want you to carry the same thing in purpose that you've been laying on in comfortability. Have you ever stopped to think how the mat got there in the first place? The same man that Jesus told to take the mat was the same person that brought it. Think about it. Nobody else there had the ability to bring the mat because of their handicap. The blind couldn't have brought it because they have no vision to see. The lame couldn't have brought it because they're crippled with injury. And you know the paralyze didn't bring it because they can't move it all.

What's your mat in life? What are you really carrying around looking for comfort in a place you don't belong? Are you comfortable being around people with no vision? Does their inability to see give you a sense of comfort from their dependency? Maybe you find comfort in being around lame people. Does their slow movement make you feel more comfortable at a pace you've set? Or better yet, maybe you're satisfied with being around the paralyzed. Their lack of movement causes anything you do to seem like progress. It doesn't matter what your mat of comfortability is, nor what group of people you find comfort in. The problem is never them, it's you. At what point in life are you going to look around and say there's more to me than where I am.

The Eagle and the Chickens

There's an old story about a farmer who found an egg in the middle of the Woods. One day an old farmer was walking through the Woods on his property and ran across an egg on the ground. It was a large egg, so the farmer picked it up to take a look at it. It didn't seem to have any cracks on it, so he decided to take it back to the farm with him. When he got back to the barn, he placed the egg in the chicken coop with the other chicken eggs. Even though the egg was much larger than the others, the chickens sat on it anyway out of natural instinct. After a few days the egg began to hatch. Much to the farmer's surprise, it was a baby eagle. The farmer had no idea what to do with the eagle, so he let it stay in the coop with the chickens. Every day the eagle got up with the chickens, walked with the chickens, ate with the chickens, and acted like a chicken. The farmer didn't see any harm with it, and the chickens thought the eagle was a part of their family.

As time went on, the eagle grew to be much larger than all the chickens around him. But nevertheless, every day he still acted like a chicken. One day, while the eagle was out in the field with the rest of the chickens, a large shadow swept across the ground. The eagle was confused because he had never seen a shadow this big moving across the ground. At the very most, he was only used to seeing the shadows of the other chickens walking around. But this was a much larger shadow sweeping across the ground. The Eagle thought, what was it? Where was it coming from? The nature of a chicken is to always look down, picking the ground for food. So, every day the eagle walked around with his head to the ground pecking for food. His whole world consisted of what he saw on the ground. He never once thought to look up to the Sky. Unexpectedly on the day that the huge shadow swept across the ground, the eagle decided to look up. When he finally looked up, he saw another eagle flying high in the sky. It was the eagle flying in front of the sun that was casting the big shadow sweeping across the ground. As the eagle on the ground looked up at the eagle flying high in the sky, the instinct within him said something is not right. He began to look down at his feet with large talons for grabbing prey. He began to stretch out his wings to feel the strength within his feathers. He was comfortable where he was, but he knew in that moment of looking in the Sky he did not belong there. All of his life he had been eating on a level beneath his ability. To make matters even worse, he had been eating alongside the very chickens that by nature were designed to feed him. He looked up at the sky and began to stretch his wings wide. With one swoop the eagle leaped from the ground into the air and began to fly! As he soared higher and higher, he began to see a whole new world from elevation that he never knew existed in isolation.

Many individuals are just like that eagle. They live their entire life beneath their ability in an environment they were never designed to thrive in. Sometimes when trying to establish the vision for your life, you must first admit there's nothing wrong with you...There's something wrong with where you are!

Chapter 6

Wake Up!

For as long as I can remember visions and dreams have always gone hand in hand. Some individuals believe you can't have one without the other. But in reality, they are actually two totally different things. A dream is a succession of images, ideas, emotions, and sensations that usually occur involuntarily in the mind during certain stages of sleep.

Dreams mainly occur in the **rapid-eye movement (REM)** stage of sleep when brain activity is high and resembles that of being awake. **REM** sleep is revealed by continuous movements of the eyes during sleep. At times, dreams may occur during other stages of sleep. However, these dreams tend to be much less vivid or memorable. The length of a dream can vary; they may last for a few seconds, or approximately 20–30 minutes. People are more likely to remember the dream if they are awakened during the **REM** phase. The average person has three to five dreams per night, and some may have up to seven; however, most dreams are immediately or quickly forgotten.

A **vision** is something seen in a dream, trance, or religious ecstasy, especially a supernatural appearance that usually conveys a revelation. Visions generally have more clarity than dreams, but traditionally fewer psychological connotations. ... Prophecy is often associated with visions.

Reality dictates that while visions are comprised of dreams, dreams are not visions. Dreams are flights of fancy. Visions are directives. When it comes to successful business, entrepreneurs are those who turn their dream into a plan. It's a vision that they make real, either as a business, a process or something entirely new and different.

Everybody has a dream of being or doing something in life. As children that was one of the first things our teacher would ask us in elementary school. What do you want to be when you grow up? There would always be a million different answers whenever the teacher would ask that question. Some kids would say I want to be a doctor or a fireman. Others would say I want to be an astronaut. If you were anything like me, I didn't have a clue of what I wanted to be when I grew up. Ironically, even though I wrote this book, I've never had a desire to be an author. Writing just seemed to come naturally with my ability to teach. Bishop TD Jakes once said, *"I never asked to be famous. I just wanted to be effective. Being famous is a byproduct of being effective."* I couldn't agree with him more.

One of the most famous dreams ever acknowledged in our lifetime is the great speech by Dr. Martin Luther King Jr., I have a dream! It's a speech about a dream that inspires hope for a nation in a time of civil rights.

Every day of your life you can look around and see the results of someone else's dream. It doesn't matter where you are nor what you're doing. You're constantly surrounded by dreams. The skyscraper towering a thousand feet in the air was an architect's dream. The beautiful car you drive was a mechanic's dream.

The amazing restaurant you dine in was a culinary chef's dream. Even down to the stylish clothes you wear was a fashion designer's dream. Every single thing in life is the result of a dream. Sadly, there's still many individuals in the world that will never make their dreams a reality.

My father used to always give me lessons in life. One of the things he would always say to me was "son, the richest place in the world is the grave. What makes the grave rich is because it's filled with dreams that died with people who never fulfilled them." That's pretty sad when you think about it. But here's the reality. There's nothing more common in the world than unsuccessful people with talent. One of the main things to keep people from pursuing their dreams is the fear of failing. Nobody wants to fail in life. But here's the secret. Failure is not the opposite of success. It's a part of it. I had to learn this lesson the hard way. There are two very important lessons that I learned from my failures.

1. **Never put your career in the hands of someone who has never had one.**
2. **Never listen to people who have never attempted to do what you failed at.**

The reality is you learned more through your failure than they could ever learn by not trying. There's an old African proverb that says never let a naked man sell you clothes. It's equivalent to trying to buy a house from a realtor that lives in an apartment. How are you going to try to sell me something that you don't even have yourself? These are powerful business concepts that many entrepreneurs use when creating a strategy for success. You may say to yourself, that sounds pretty simple. Well, if it was really that simple, why aren't there more successful people pursuing their dreams? I'm glad you asked.

So far in this chapter I've been dealing with the concept of dreams. The problem isn't your dream. The problem is the state that you're in while you're dreaming. You see the first step to making any one of your dreams come true is you must wake up! As long as you're dreaming, you're still asleep. Wake up, turn your dream into a vision and turn your vision into a plan. It's an old cliche, but it's the truth. If you fail to plan, then you plan to fail. Wake up! Don't just waste your life dreaming in a state of sleep. Get up and turn that dream into a vision. Do you know what the Bible says about sleep?

NIV Proverbs Chapter 20 verse 13

Do not love sleep or you will grow poor; stay awake and you will have food to spare.

NIV Proverbs Chapter 24 verses 33-34

[33] A little sleep, a little slumber,
a little folding of the hands to rest—
[34] and poverty will come on you like a thief
and scarcity like an armed man.

You don't have any less time in the day than a millionaire does. There are 24 hours in a day and 168 hours in a week. What are you doing with your time? What are you doing with your dreams? Are you still sleep? When are you going to wake up and put a plan into action? Successful individuals do not waste time giving excuses. Do you know what an excuse is? An excuse is the skin of a lie. And procrastination are the shoes worn on the feet of failure. Wake up! It's bad enough that people go to sleep every night with a dream and wake up and do nothing with it. But it's even worst to walk around awake with dreams and still be asleep in life.

How to catch a Moose

Over the years I've been blessed to sit in different rooms with millionaires. Whenever I find myself in the company of someone with great success, I always ask them questions. One day I was sitting at a table having a conversation with a millionaire and I asked him a simple question. How do I become a millionaire? His response was totally unexpected and left me very confused. He said, "figure out how to catch a moose." Huh? What do you mean figure out how to catch a moose? I looked at him and said, what does that have anything to do with becoming a millionaire? He said, "if you figure out how to catch a moose, then you'll learn how to become a millionaire." Seeing that I was totally confused with a smirk on his face, he said, let me explain. If you're going to catch a moose, the first thing you have to do is find out where they are. I live in Virginia, so the odds of me seeing a moose here is virtually none. As a matter of fact, you can't even find any moose on the entire East Coast of the United States. You have to go to Alaska. He said after you figure out where they are then you have to find out what paths and trails they take. Understanding the steps they take and the different paths they walk in life are very essential to you catching a moose. He then went on to say, next you need to figure out what do they have an appetite for? What do they like to eat? What do they feed on daily? And finally, he said, do you have something big enough to hold it? If by chance you do catch one, do you have the capacity to hold the weight of something that big? He looked at me and said, Jon, if you can figure out all of this, then you'll figure out how to become a millionaire.

You see, the story was never really about the moose. The moose was simply a metaphor used for millionaires. The story was about understanding the characteristics of a millionaire and the daily routines they practice in life.

Your dream is an amazing gift that God gives to you. It serves as a glimpse into the future of what you could have. It surpasses the limitations of your present point of view and shows you a life of possibilities. Don't let your dreams die in the grave. There's much more to you than anyone could imagine. Sometimes our biggest challenge in life is simply getting past the person we see in the mirror. Even though you may not verbally speak it out loud, thinking negative thoughts can be detrimental to your vision. Believe in yourself and the dream that God has given you. You don't have to be an expert to produce quality. Some of the greatest things we experience in the world today were created by people who were considered amateurs. I mean after all, amateurs built the Ark while professionals built the Titanic. And we all know how that story turned out. You already have within you everything you need to change what you see around you. All you have to do is simply wake up and make your dream a reality. The next time you get up, take a look in the mirror and ask yourself this question...... What's the purpose of having sight if you can't see with vision?

In loving memory of Larry Brown

Made in the USA
Columbia, SC
07 September 2022

66623901R00033